Moseley

Games & Gadgets for the Church School

Games & Gadgets for the Church School

Donna Skinner

Publishing House
St. Louis

Bible quotations are from the King James or Authorized Version of the Bible.

Hasbro Industries has graciously given permission to include games using Lite-Brite® in this book.

3558 S. Jefferson Avenue, St. Louis, MO 63118
Manufactured in the United States of America

Library of Congress Cataloging in Publication Data

Skinner, Donna.
Games and gadgets for the church school.

1. Games in Christian education. I. Title.
BV1536.3.S58 1983 268'.6 83-7572
ISBN 0-570-03914-2 (pbk.)

1 2 3 4 5 6 7 8 9 10 WMP 92 91 90 89 88 87 86 85 84 83

To Jesus,
who gave me
a loving Christian mother

CONTENTS

INTRODUCTION

God built a love for play into every child. A child's intellectual and creative abilities flower as he or she explores the world of make believe. A child learns to be assertive, to share, to experiment, and to make decisions when he or she plays a game. Because a child learns while he plays, and loves doing it; play is an excellent tool to utilize in the educational process. A child with a negative attitude about learning will perk up when he hears a game is to be played. That the game is a learning tool is secondary. He or she will participate eagerly if the game is suited to his or her age level and abilities.

As teachers we have a responsibility to make learning interesting, to create in a child a hunger to know more. We all know that one presentation isn't enough for most children to understand what we are teaching. We spend much of our time "reteaching." This can be boring. Or it can be a challenge, an exciting, fun-filled experience, especially if we incorporate games and other activities.

- A game has built in motivation. It allows each child to participate in the activity.
- Games provide growth in the social awareness of a child. They allow a child to experience success and to cope with disappointment. A child learns to try new approaches and to accept the consequences of his or her choices. A child learns to be generous, to share, to take turns, and to talk to others as he or she plays.
- Games teach a child to follow directions.
- They provide follow-up and reinforcement.

When preparing games, your primary goal should be KEEP IT SIMPLE:

- Establish goals you expect the children to reach.
- Give clear instructions.
- Provide a method for self-checking.
- The game should be easy enough to be fun, yet hard enough to be a challenge.
- Provide different levels of difficulty.

Try the games and activities in this book, but don't be afraid to make up your own. It's a wonderful way for children to make their own discoveries and to increase their understanding of the Bible. It's a new way to learn every Sunday.

Our children find God's world one of wonder and discovery. They are full of energy and express a constant need for activity. A teacher must manage this energy rather than try to stop it. You certainly can't keep up with it. We must use this strength and energy to make learning God's word fun and exciting.

The purpose of GAMES AND GADGETS is to help you direct this energy so your children's needs can be met—while enriching the content of your curriculum.

CARD GAMES

This section includes instructions for 11 card games. Follow the directions and make dozens of games that cover a wide variety of subjects.

Method 1

1. Choose a subject. Use a Bible dictionary to locate short biographies of Bible people, definitions of Bible words, or names of Bible places and what happened there.
2. Mark off the required number of cards on poster board.
3. With felt-tipped markers, print on the cards the information you have gathered. (Children love lots of different colors.)
4. Include an extra card with the instructions.
5. Cover the back of the cards with colorful contact paper.
6. Laminate the information side and cut the cards apart.

Method 2

1. Choose a subject as you did for method 1.
2. Type the information on paper that has been divided into blocks a quarter inch smaller than a playing card.
3. Cut apart.
4. Use rubber cement to glue the paper cards to the numbered side of the playing cards.
5. Laminate the playing side.

True or False Button Drop

For Two or More Children

Preparations

Make a deck of 24 cards that list 12 true statements and 12 false statements from the Bible. The game is played by the following rules:

1. Pass out a different colored button to each child.
2. Place a small bowl or cup in the center of the table.
3. Shuffle the deck and place the cards face down on the table.
4. Turn the cards over one at a time.
5. If the statement is true, the children must put their buttons into the cup.
6. The child who is the first to put his or her button into the cup receives the card.
7. The players retrieve their buttons and get ready for the next card to be turned over.
8. The child who has the most "true" cards when all the cards have been turned over wins the game.

The next four games can be played with a single set of cards, so make several sets that feature different subjects. Sample cards for "Who Am I" are included. The New Testament and the Old Testament are the subjects of these sample cards. You can focus on the disciples; the early church; or perhaps Bible places, Bible foods, Bible occupations, or Bible animals.

Match Two, Throw One Away

For Two or More Children

Preparations

Make 24 cards with words from the Bible on the first 12 and their definitions on the remainder. You may also use people biographies, half a Scripture verse on each card, or questions and answers. Familiar pictures that match a Bible-story title are fun for younger children.

Playing Instructions

1. Deal five cards.
2. Put the remainder of the cards in a draw pile.
3. The object of the game is to match a word and its definition.
4. If you have two cards that match, lay them down.
5. Each time a match is made, the person may discard an extra card from his or her hand. This is the only time a player may throw away a card.
6. Other players may challenge your match. If the match is wrong, you must return the cards to your hand and draw another card from the deck.
7. When it is your turn, you must draw from the deck or the discard pile.
8. The first player to discard all of his or her cards wins the game.

Remember This

For Two or Three Children

Preparations

Prepare this game as you did "Match Two, Throw One Away."

Playing Instructions

1. Lay the "name" cards face down in a pattern of four cards in three rows, as shown in the diagram.
2. Lay the 12 "definition" cards face down in the same manner.
3. Take turns picking up and turning over one of the definition cards.
4. Choose one name card, turn it over and see if you have a match.
5. If a match is made, place the cards on your side of the table.
6. If a match isn't made, return the name card face down to its previous position on the table.
7. The first person to pair all of his or her cards wins the game.

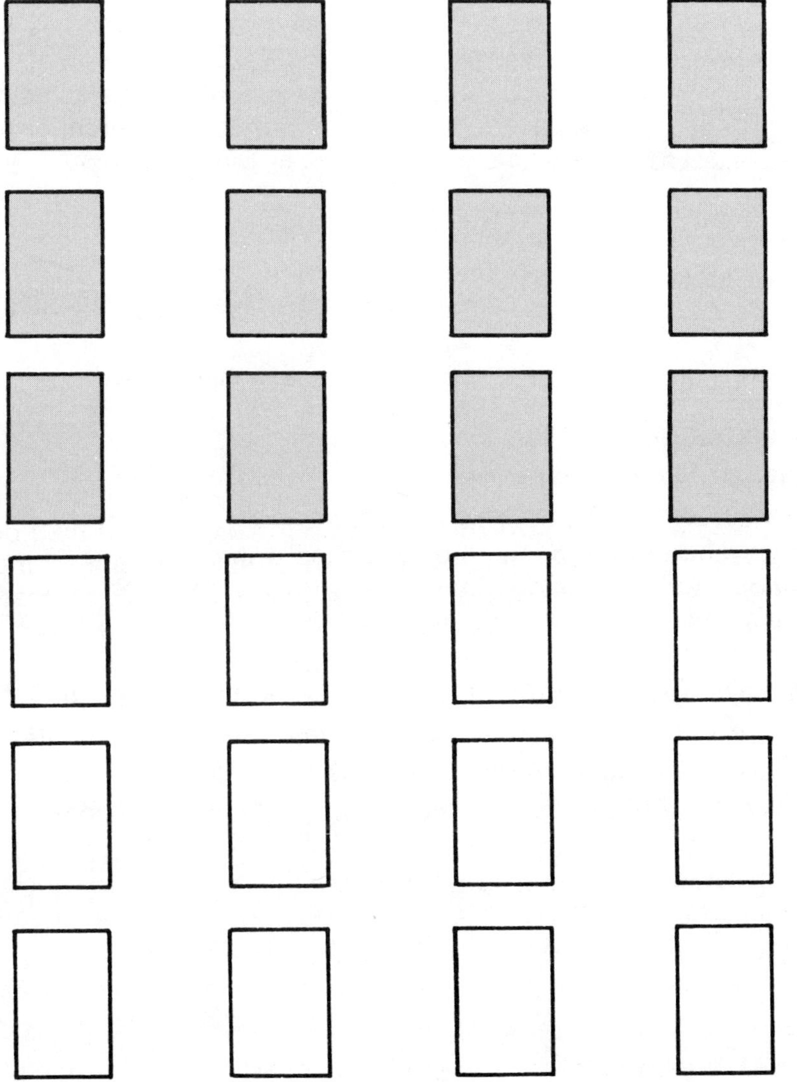

Know It or Throw It

For Two or Three Children

Preparations
Prepare this game as you did "Match Two, Throw One Away."

Playing Instructions
1. Lay the 12 "name" cards face up on the table so that each one is visible.
2. Lay the 12 "definition" cards face down as a draw pile.
3. Take turns drawing a card and trying to match it to one of the name cards. If you don't know the answer, discard.
4. If a match is made, pick up the pair and keep it.
5. The next player may draw from the deck or the discard pile.
6. When all of the cards have been matched, the person with the most pairs wins the game.

Who Am I?

For Two or More Children

Preparations
Prepare this game as you did "Match Two, Throw One Away."

Playing Instructions
1. Shuffle the cards.
2. Deal out all cards as evenly as possible.
3. Each player must try to match biographies with characters (or words with definitions, etc.) by asking other players for the character card that matches a biography card in his hand. (He must ask for the character by name.)
4. If the player has the card that was named, he must give it up.
5. The player's turn continues as long as the player asked has the card.
6. The player loses his or her turn when he or she fails to receive a card.
7. The first player to match all of his or her cards wins the game.

Moses	Joshua	Samuel
Samson	David	Daniel
Abraham	Noah	Jonah
Joseph	Isaac	Jacob

If you cut out these cards along with those on page 17, you will have a sample version of the Old Testament game "Who Am I?" See the directions on page 11 for making cards.

An Egyptian princess found him in a little boat and raised him as her own son. He led the Israelites across the Red Sea. Exodus 2:1-10; 14	This man was Moses' special helper. He led the people into the Promised Land to capture the city of Jericho. Exodus 24:13 Joshua 6	His mother gave him to the Lord when he was a young boy. He became a judge. He anointed Saul and David to be kings of Israel. 1 Samuel 1:11,22,24—28
A Nazarite, a prophet, and a judge of Israel, this man was given special strength from God. He lost that strength when he told Delilah his secret. Judges 16	As a shepherd boy he killed a lion, a bear, and a giant. He became a great King. 1 Samuel 17:34-36 2 Samuel 5:4-5	He was a Jewish captive of the Babylonians. He obeyed God even when threatened with the lions' den. Daniel 1:6; 6
God made a promise to this man. If he was obedient, God would give him the Promised Land and many descendants. Later, God changed his name. Genesis 12:1-3; 17:5	God looked at the earth and saw only one righteous man. God told this man to build an ark and take his family and two of each kind of animal on board to escape the Flood. Genesis 6:14-22	God told this man to warn the people of Nineveh to change their evil ways. He ran away from God and was swallowed by a great fish. Jonah 1
He was Jacob's favorite son. He was sold into slavery by his jealous brothers. He rose to a position of power in Egypt after he interpreted Pharoah's dreams. Genesis 37:3-4,26-28; 41:39-40	He was born to Abraham and Sarah when they were very old. Abraham was willing to sacrifice him because God told him to do so. Genesis 21:1-3; 22:1-19	He was the brother of Esau. Isaac and Rebekah were his parents. He tricked his brother and his father. Genesis 25; 27:1-29

One, Two, Three, Four, Five

For Four Players

Preparations

1. Make a set of 20 cards. Divide the cards into four sets.
2. Choose four Bible stories. Write the title of story 1 on a card from the first set. Write the title of story 2 on a card from the second set—and so on.
3. Write four sentences that tell the story of Bible Story 1. Put one sentence on each remaining card of the set. (A set will include the title and four sentence cards.) Repeat the procedure for Bible Stories 2—4.
4. For younger children, use five pictures that depict the sequence of the story.

Playing Instructions

1. Each player shuffles his five cards.
2. At the signal to start, each player puts his cards in order as fast as he can.
3. The winner is the first player to finish.

Bible Disciples

For Two to Four Players

Preparations

Make a set of 40 cards.

1. Choose four Bible characters or stories.
2. For character 1 (or story 1), write five sentences that describe the character or tell the story. Put one sentence on each card. Write the character's name or the story title on the remaining five cards. (You will need five sentence cards and five name cards for each character or story.)
3. Do the same for characters 2—4.

Playing Instructions

1. Shuffle the name cards and the sentence cards separately.
2. Each player is dealt five name cards. If you have fewer than four players, you won't need the additional cards, so lay them aside.
3. The sentence cards are shuffled and placed in a draw pile. Turn the top card face up.
4. You may choose the face-up card or draw a card.
5. Try to pair your name cards with the biography cards.
6. Lay down any pairs and go to the next turn. If you do not have a match, place the "biography" card on the discard pile.
7. The first person to lay down all of his or her cards wins the game.
8. Any player may challenge another about the cards he or she had laid

down as a pair. If a player is challenged correctly, the challenger may discard any name card in his hand.

9. A player who has mismatched a pair, loses a turn and may not discard. He must return the name card to his hand and put the biography card on the discard pile.
10. If all of the cards are taken from the draw pile before the game ends, pick up the cards from the discard pile and follow instruction 3 above. Continue until a player has won.

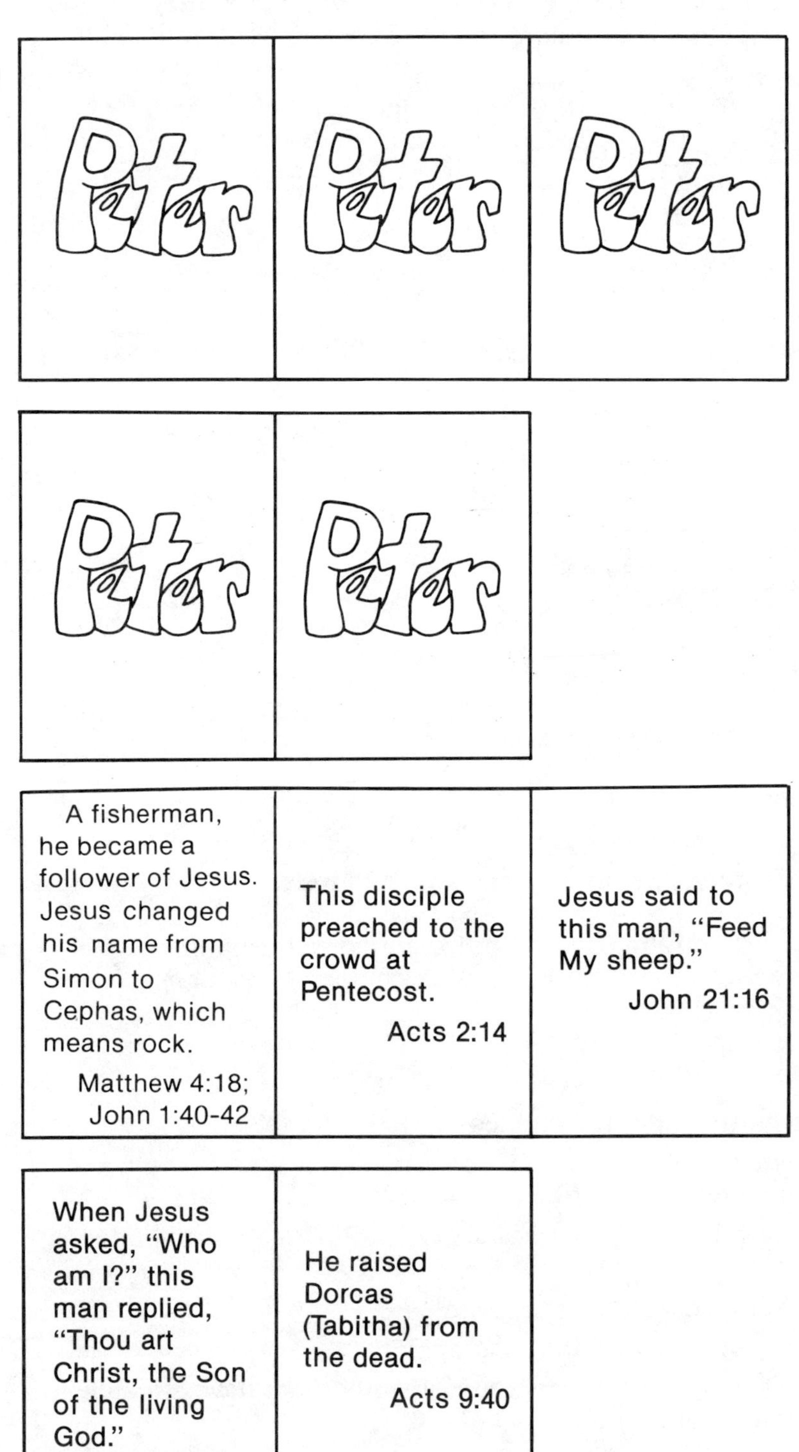

The cards for "Bible Disciples" might look like those illustrated on this page.

The playing cards for a "parables" version of "Bible Disciples" might look like the cards illustrated here. For "One, Two, Three . . ." only one name card and four sentence cards would be required.

A man who had 100 sheep lost one in the wilderness.
Luke 15:3-7
Matthew 18:12-14

The shepherd left the 99 sheep and went out to look for the one that was lost.
Luke 15:3-7
Matthew 18:12-14

When he found the lost sheep, he was very happy. He carried it home on his shoulders.
Luke 15:3-7
Matthew 18:12-14

The shepherd was so happy that he called all his friends and neighbors together to rejoice with him.
Luke 15:3-7
Matthew 18:12-14

In the same way, our Father in heaven is not willing that any of His children should be lost.
Luke 15:3-7
Matthew 18:12-14

Draw One More

For Two or Three Children

Preparations

Prepare a deck of 66 cards that list the books of the Bible (three Bible books to a card; three cards to a suit). Mark each card with a large number as shown in the samples following these directions. (Or you may transfer these samples to poster board. See the directions at the beginning of this section.)

Playing Instructions

1. Shuffle the cards.
2. Deal the cards, one at a time, to the left. If two or three are playing, deal seven cards. If four or five are playing, deal five cards.
3. Turn the remaining cards face down for the draw pile.
4. The first child begins by saying, for example, "Give me your *Genesis Exodus, Leviticus* card." (The player must have at least one card of that kind in his hand.)
5. The player questioned must hand over any cards he has of that description.
6. If he doesn't have the card, he answers, "Draw one more." The player asking for the card must then draw from the pile.
7. When a player has three of a kind, he or she has a match and can lay the cards down.
8. If the player gets a card when he asks for it, he may continue asking as long as he receives a card when he asks.
9. If, when told to draw one, he gets the card from the draw pile, he continues his turn.
10. The game ends when all the cards have been matched. The player with the most matched sets wins the game.

If you cut out the cards at the bottom of this page as well as those on pages 23—35, you will have a version of the cards for "Draw One More." See the directions on page 11 for making cards.

The cards for "Draw One More" might look like the cards illustrated here.

2 Numbers Deuteronomy Joshua 2	2 Numbers Deuteronomy Joshua 2	2 Numbers Deuteronomy Joshua 2
3 Judges Ruth I Samuel 3	3 Judges Ruth I Samuel 3	3 Judges Ruth I Samuel 3
4 II Samuel I Kings II Kings 4	4 II Samuel I Kings II Kings 4	4 II Samuel I Kings II Kings 4

5 I Chronicles II Chronicles Ezra 5	5 I Chronicles II Chronicles Ezra 5	5 I Chronicles II Chronicles Ezra 5
6 Nehemiah Esther Job 6	6 Nehemiah Esther Job 6	6 Nehemiah Esther Job 6
7 Psalms Proverbs Ecclesiastes 7	7 Psalms Proverbs Ecclesiastes 7	7 Psalms Proverbs Ecclesiastes 7

8 Song of Solomon Isaiah Jeremiah 8	8 Song of Solomon Isaiah Jeremiah 8	8 Song of Solomon Isaiah Jeremiah 8
9 Lamentations Ezekiel Daniel 9	9 Lamentations Ezekiel Daniel 9	9 Lamentations Ezekiel Daniel 9
10 Hosea Joel Amos 10	10 Hosea Joel Amos 10	10 Hosea Joel Amos 10

11 Obadiah Jonah Micah 11	11 Obadiah Jonah Micah 11	11 Obadiah Jonah Micah 11
12 Nahum Habakkuk Zephaniah 12	12 Nahum Habakkuk Zephaniah 12	12 Nahum Habakkuk Zephaniah 12
13 Haggai Zechariah Malachi 13	13 Haggai Zechariah Malachi 13	13 Haggai Zechariah Malachi 13

14 Matthew Mark Luke 14	14 Matthew Mark Luke 14	14 Matthew Mark Luke 14
15 John Acts Romans 15	15 John Acts Romans 15	15 John Acts Romans 15
16 I Corinthians II Corinthians Galatians 16	16 I Corinthians II Corinthians Galatians 16	16 I Corinthians II Corinthians Galatians 16

17 Ephesians Philippians Colossians 17	17 Ephesians Philippians Colossians 17	17 Ephesians Philippians Colossians 17
18 I Thessalonians II Thessalonians I Timothy 18	18 I Thessalonians II Thessalonians I Timothy 18	18 I Thessalonians II Thessalonians I Timothy 18
19 II Timothy Titus Philemon 19	19 II Timothy Titus Philemon 19	19 II Timothy Titus Philemon 19

20 Hebrews James I Peter 20	20 Hebrews James I Peter 20	20 Hebrews James I Peter 20
21 II Peter I John II John 21	21 II Peter I John II John 21	21 II Peter I John II John 21
22 III John Jude Revelation 22	22 III John Jude Revelation 22	22 III John Jude Revelation 22

File a Book

For Two or More Children

Preparations

1. Make a total of 132 cards.
2. Write the name of a Bible book on each of 66 cards.
3. Prepare the remaining 66 cards as follows:
   - 13 cards—history
   - 5 cards—law
   - 5 cards—poetry and wisdom
   - 12 cards—minor prophets
   - 5 cards—major prophets
   - 4 cards—gospels
   - 13 cards—epistles of Paul
   - 8 cards—general epistles
   - 1 card—prophesy
4. Prepare a poster that shows the major divisions of the Bible. Display it near the playing area the first few times the children play this game.

Playing Instructions

1. Shuffle and deal 12 cards to each player.
2. Lay down any pairs you may have; pairs consist of a book of the Bible matched with its proper category.
3. A player may draw two cards each time it is his turn. All pairs must be laid down each turn.
4. If a player lays down all cards, he must draw a new hand of 12 cards.
5. After the draw pile is consumed, the players must take turns drawing a card from the person on the left.
6. The drawing continues until there are no more cards and all matches have been made.
7. The person with the most matches wins the game.

Bible Solitaire 1

Preparations

Make 40 cards. On 20 of the cards, write the name of a Bible character. On the other 20, write a short biography of that character or a fact about that character. (Other subjects, such as Bible places, may be used also.)

Playing Instructions

1. Lay the cards, face up, in the pattern shown in the diagram.
2. The remainder of the cards are the deck.
3. Turn up one card at a time. If the card matches one of the cards on the table, they are paired and removed.

4. Unplayable cards are stacked face up on the table.
5. The player is allowed to go through the deck one time.
6. All face-up cards in the pattern must be discarded to win.

Bible Solitaire 2

Preparations

Follow the directions for making "Bible Solitaire 1."

Playing Instructions

1. Lay the cards out in the following manner: One down, one up in the first pile. Two down, one up in the second stack. Three down, one up in the third, four down, one up in the fourth, and five down, one up in the fifth stack.
2. The remainder of the cards comprise the deck and are left face down.
3. Turn the cards in the deck over, three at a time, and try to match the cards that are face up on the table with the third of the three cards that have been turned over.
4. Remove those cards that match and turn the card underneath up.
5. The player may go through the deck three times.
6. If he has used all of the deck, he wins the game.

Sample cards for a Bible places version of "Bible Solitaire."

Tarsus	Paul was born here. He returned to this place when he was threatened for preaching about Jesus. Barnabus went to this city to ask Paul to go with him to Antioch to preach. Acts 9:11–30; 11:25–26
Ur	This was Abraham's birthplace. It is believed to be one of the first cities built after the flood. Genesis 11:28

OPEN-ENDED GAME BOARDS

Game boards are easy to make. Use them any time, for any subject.

You will need: Poster board, felt-tipped markers, game board patterns, paper, Bible questions, die

Game Board 1

Preparations

1. Remove and transfer the game board to poster board.
2. Laminate the game.
3. Use a box knife to cut out the spaces marked with a ?.
4. Lay two sheets of white paper under the game board and write the questions in the empty spaces.
5. Paper clip the questions to the game board.

OR

1. (Same as above.)
2. (Same as above.)
3. On 3-by-5 cards prepare a series of questions relating to the topic you are studying. These will be used when a player lands on a space marked with a ?.

How to Use

1. The player must throw a three or a one to begin playing.
2. Throw the die and move the number of spaces indicated on the die.
3. Follow the directions of the space on which you land. If you land on a space with a question (or one marked with a ?), you must answer that question correctly or lose your next turn. (If the question is answered incorrectly, be sure the players know the correct answer to the question before you proceed with the game.)

Game Board 1

You goofed! Go back to 8.

You slept through your turn!

Go to 23.

It's a toughie, but you can do it! Go to 11.

Dead end! Go that way!

How to Use

1. The player must throw a three or a one to begin playing.
2. Throw the die and move the number of spaces indicated on the die.
3. Follow the directions of the space on which you land. If you land on a space with a question (or one marked with a ?), you must answer that question correctly or lose your next turn.

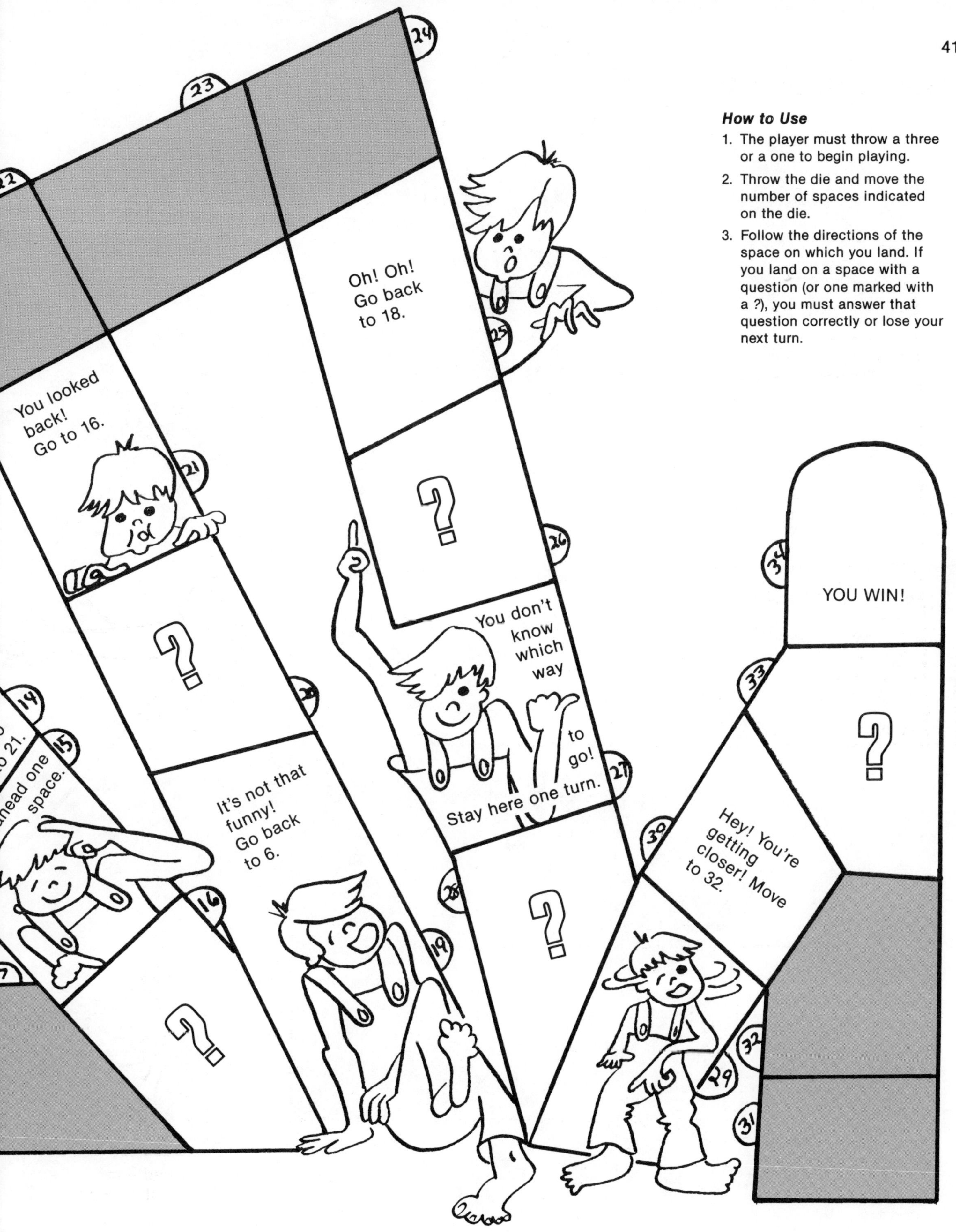

Game Board 2

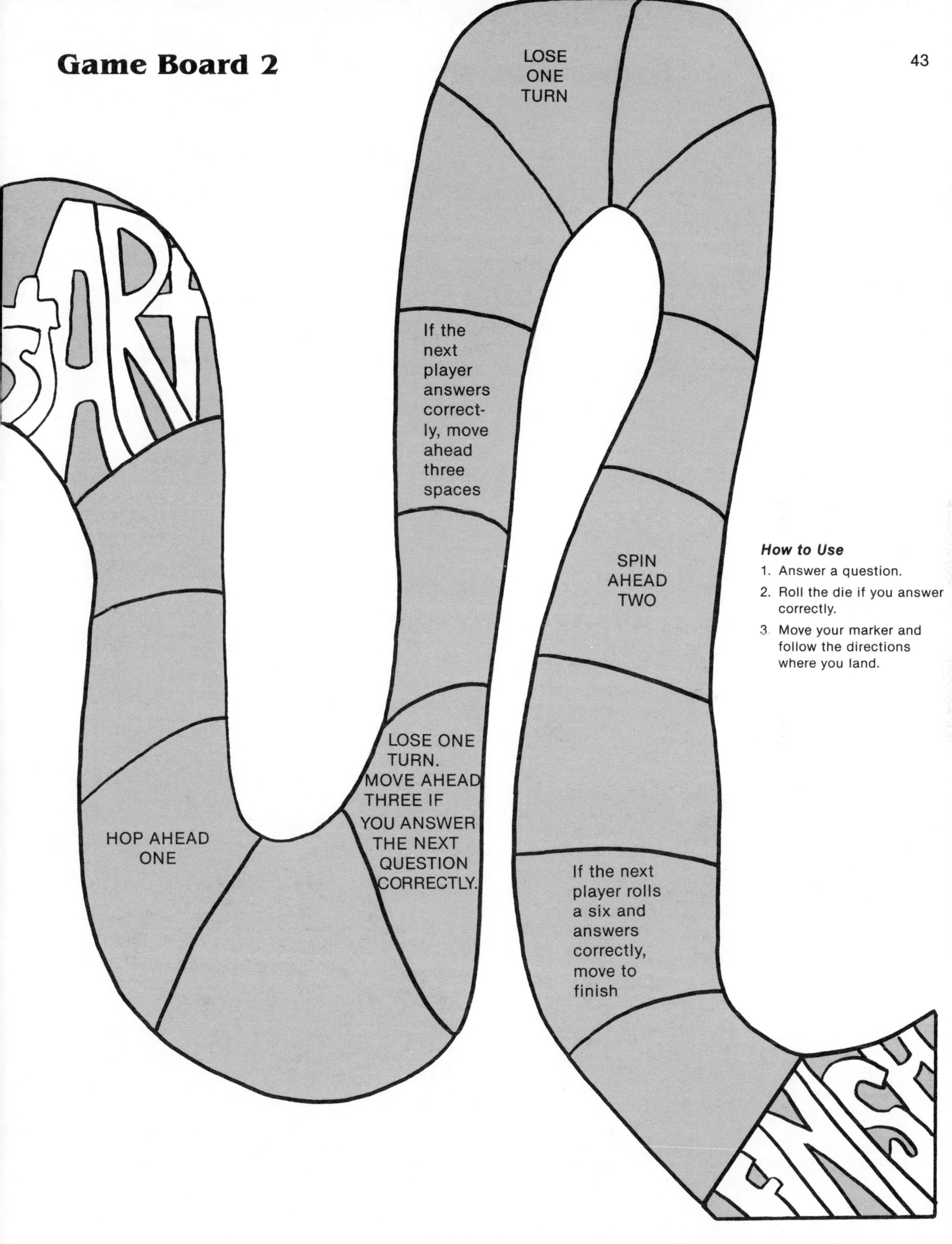

How to Use

1. Answer a question.
2. Roll the die if you answer correctly.
3. Move your marker and follow the directions where you land.

Game Board 2

Remove and transfer game board to poster board. Laminate.

Game Board 3

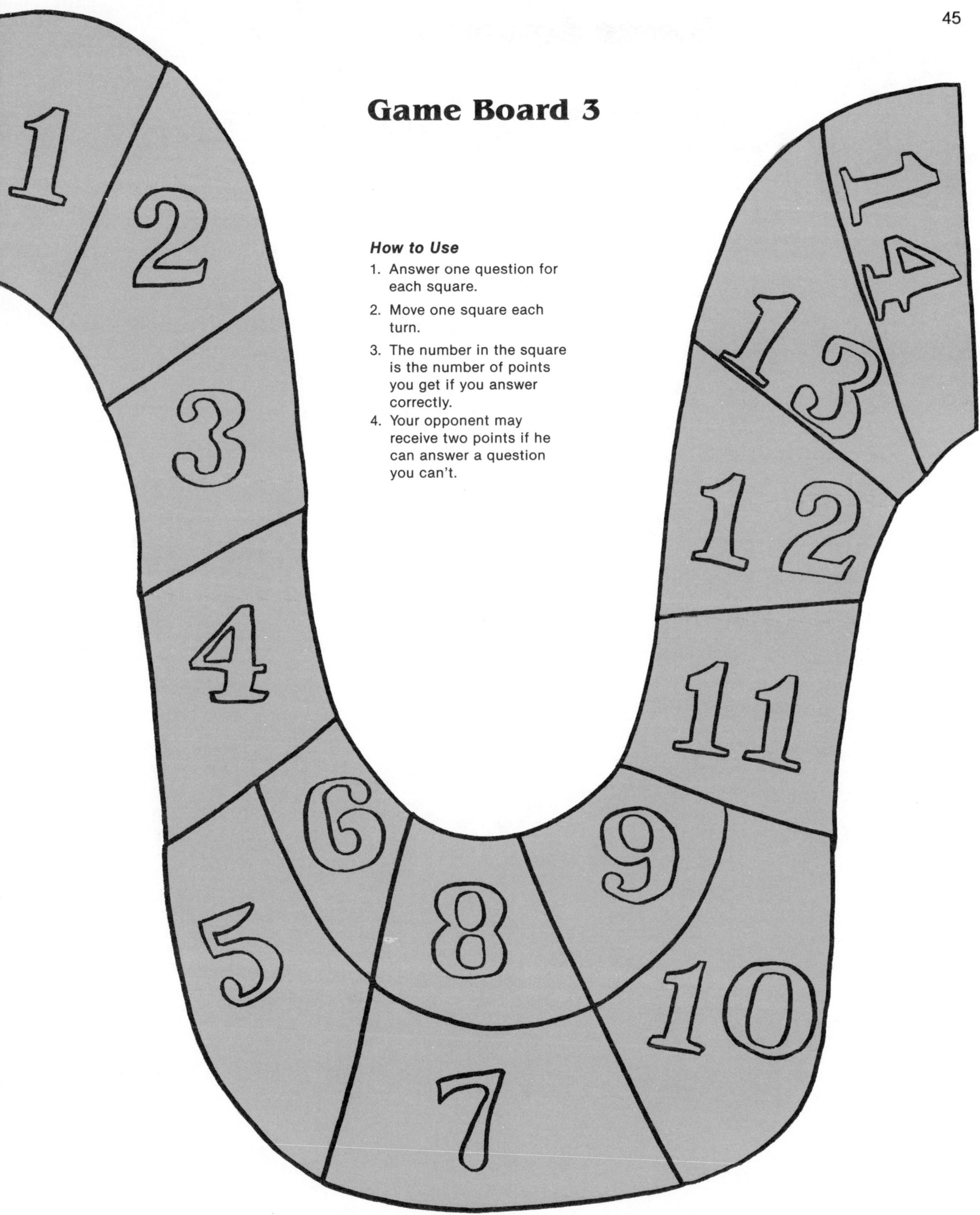

How to Use

1. Answer one question for each square.
2. Move one square each turn.
3. The number in the square is the number of points you get if you answer correctly.
4. Your opponent may receive two points if he can answer a question you can't.

Game Board 3

Remove and transfer game board to poster board. Laminate.

STORY WHEELS AND QUESTION WHEELS

You will need: question- or story-wheel patterns, poster board, brads, felt-tipped markers

Preparations

1. Cut out and transfer the patterns to sturdy poster board.
2. Color the pictures.
3. Laminate.
4. For the question wheel, place the brads through points A and B. For the story wheel, place brads through points A, B, C, and D of the flowers and through the "base" of the story wheel.

A Story Wheel

How to Use the Story Wheel

1. Spin wheels A, B, and C to determine character, setting, and problem.
2. Write a story using that information.
3. Turn wheel D to a verse you think would best go with your story.
4. Write that verse at the end of your story.

Assembled story wheel

D C

Detach full sheet.

B A

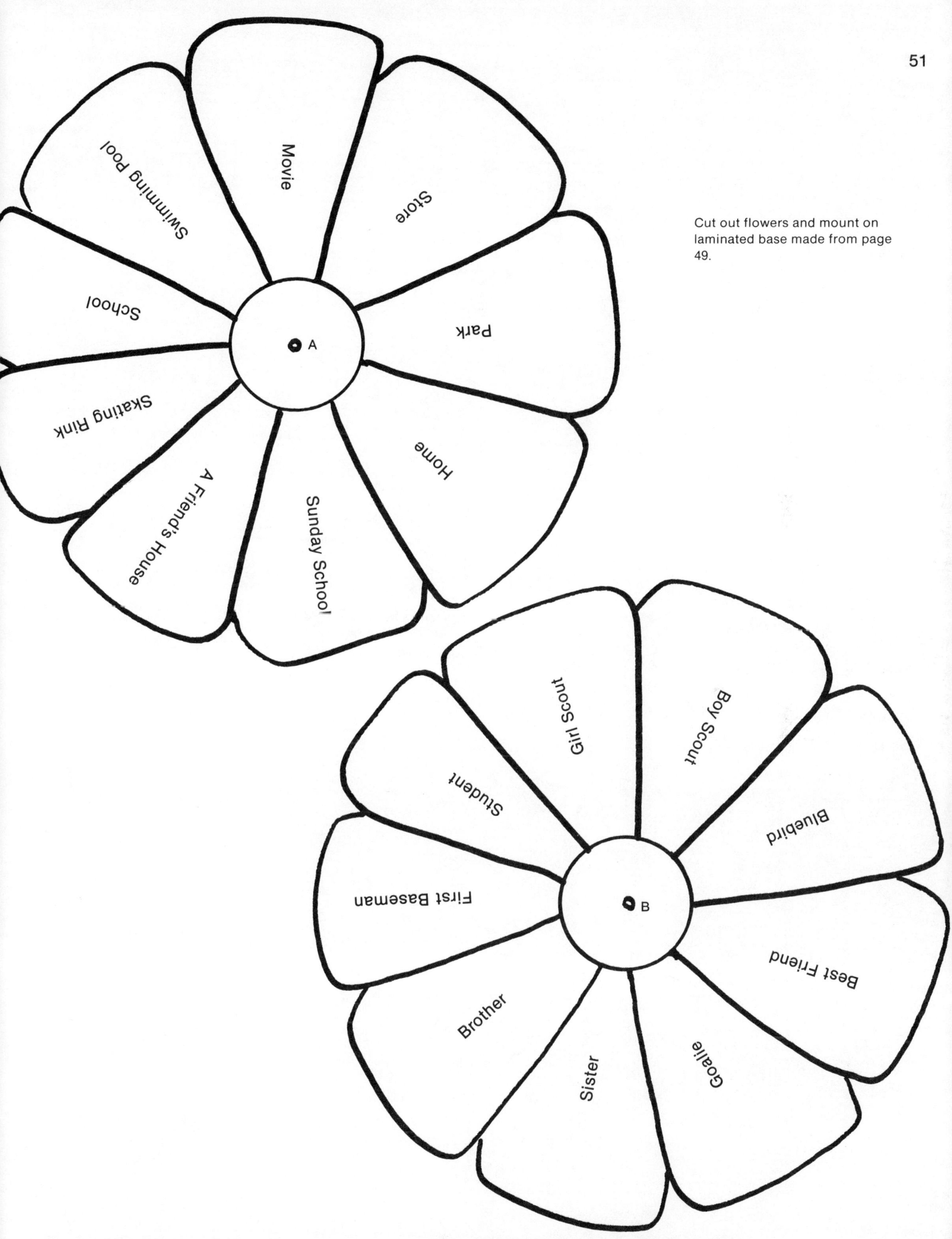

Cut out flowers and mount on laminated base made from page 49.

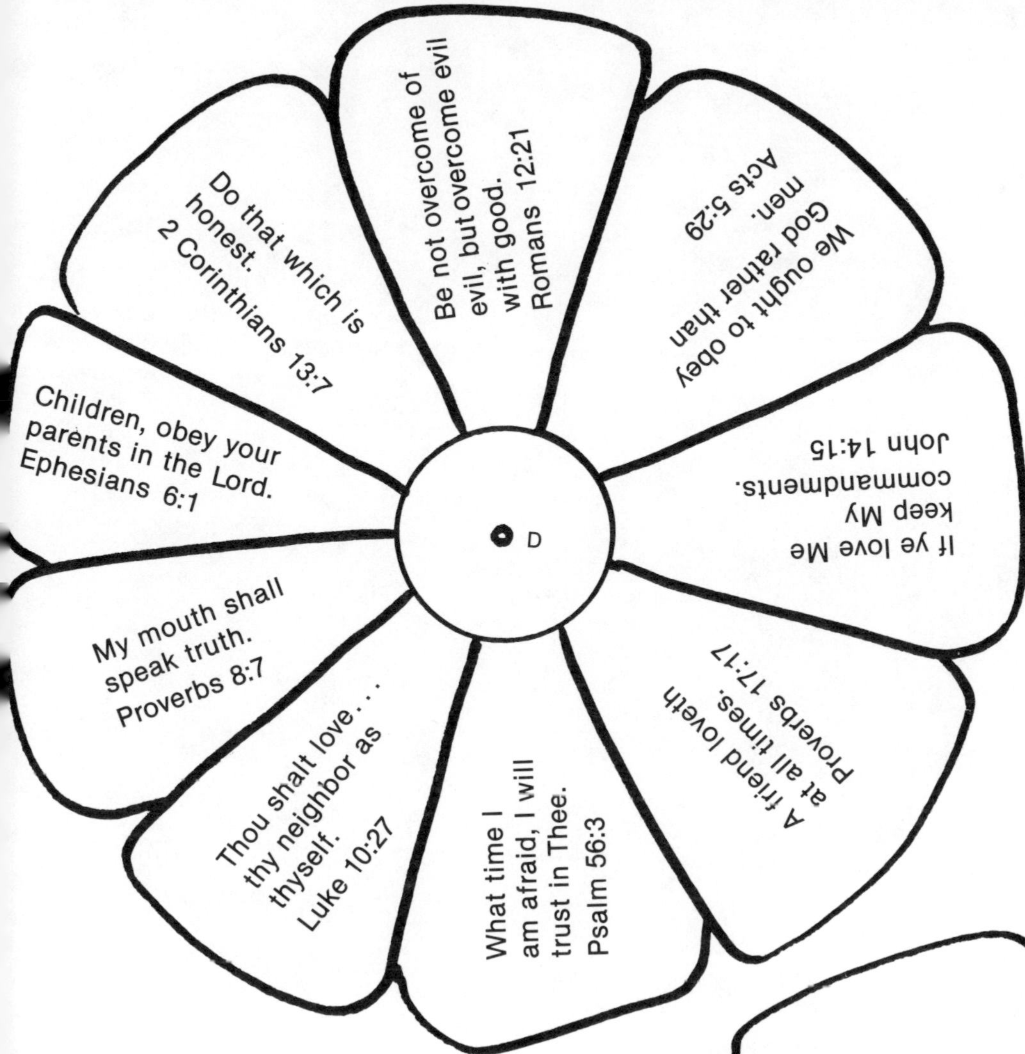

D

Be not overcome of evil, but overcome evil with good. Romans 12:21

We ought to obey God rather than men. Acts 5:29

If ye love Me keep My commandments. John 14:15

A friend loveth at all times. Proverbs 17:17

What time I am afraid, I will trust in Thee. Psalm 56:3

Thou shalt love . . . thy neighbor as thyself. Luke 10:27

My mouth shall speak truth. Proverbs 8:7

Children, obey your parents in the Lord. Ephesians 6:1

Do that which is honest. 2 Corinthians 13:7

C

Telling a Lie

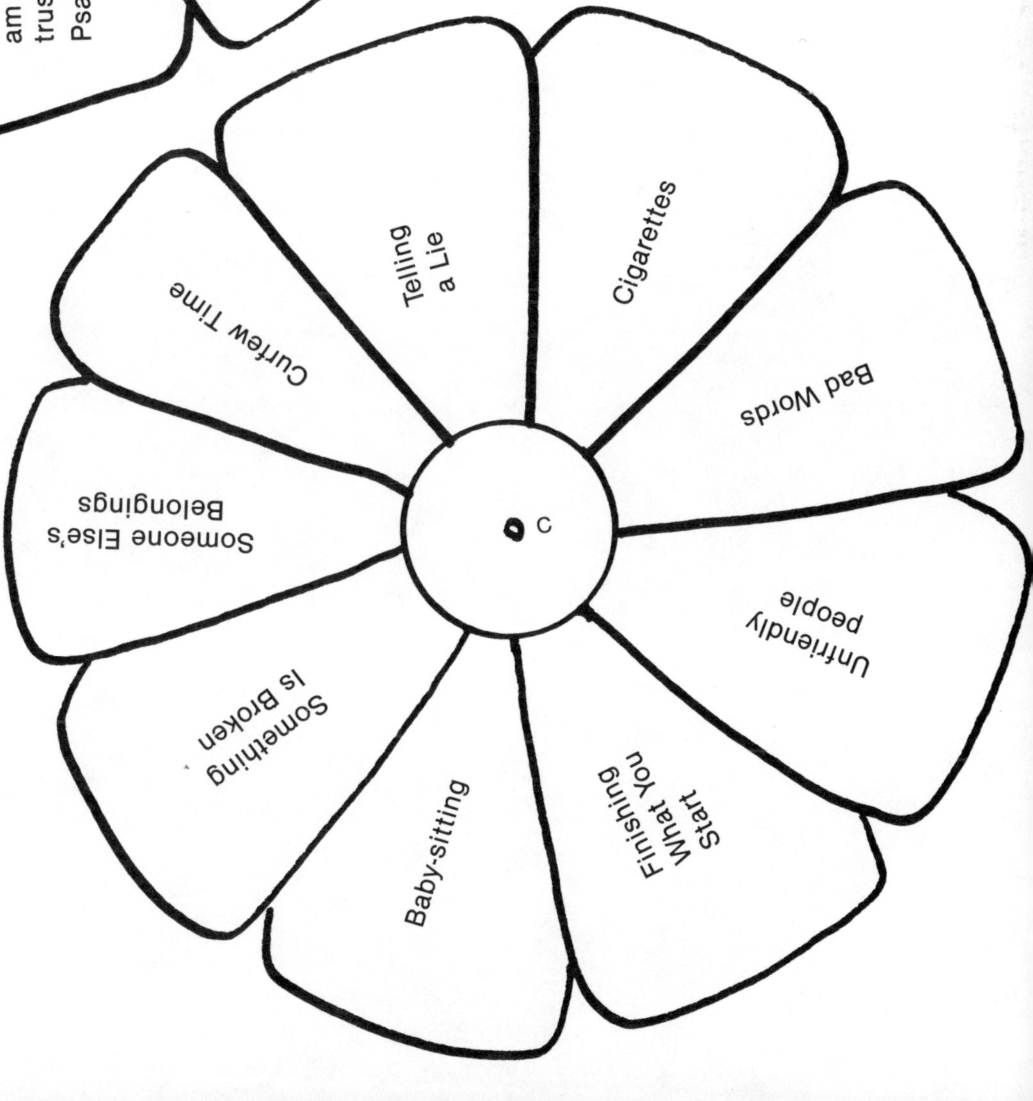

Cigarettes

Bad Words

Unfriendly people

Finishing What You Start

Baby-sitting

Something is Broken

Someone Else's Belongings

Curfew Time

A Noah Question Wheel

How to Use the Question Wheel

1. The wheel can be used by two children.
2. Child 1 holds the wheel and selects a question to ask child 2. When child 2 answers the question, the first child can check whether the answer is correct.
3. The players may take turns asking and answering questions. (The answer to the question may be covered up by moving the head of the elephant over the answer window.)
4. The game may also be played by more than two children.

Assembled question wheel

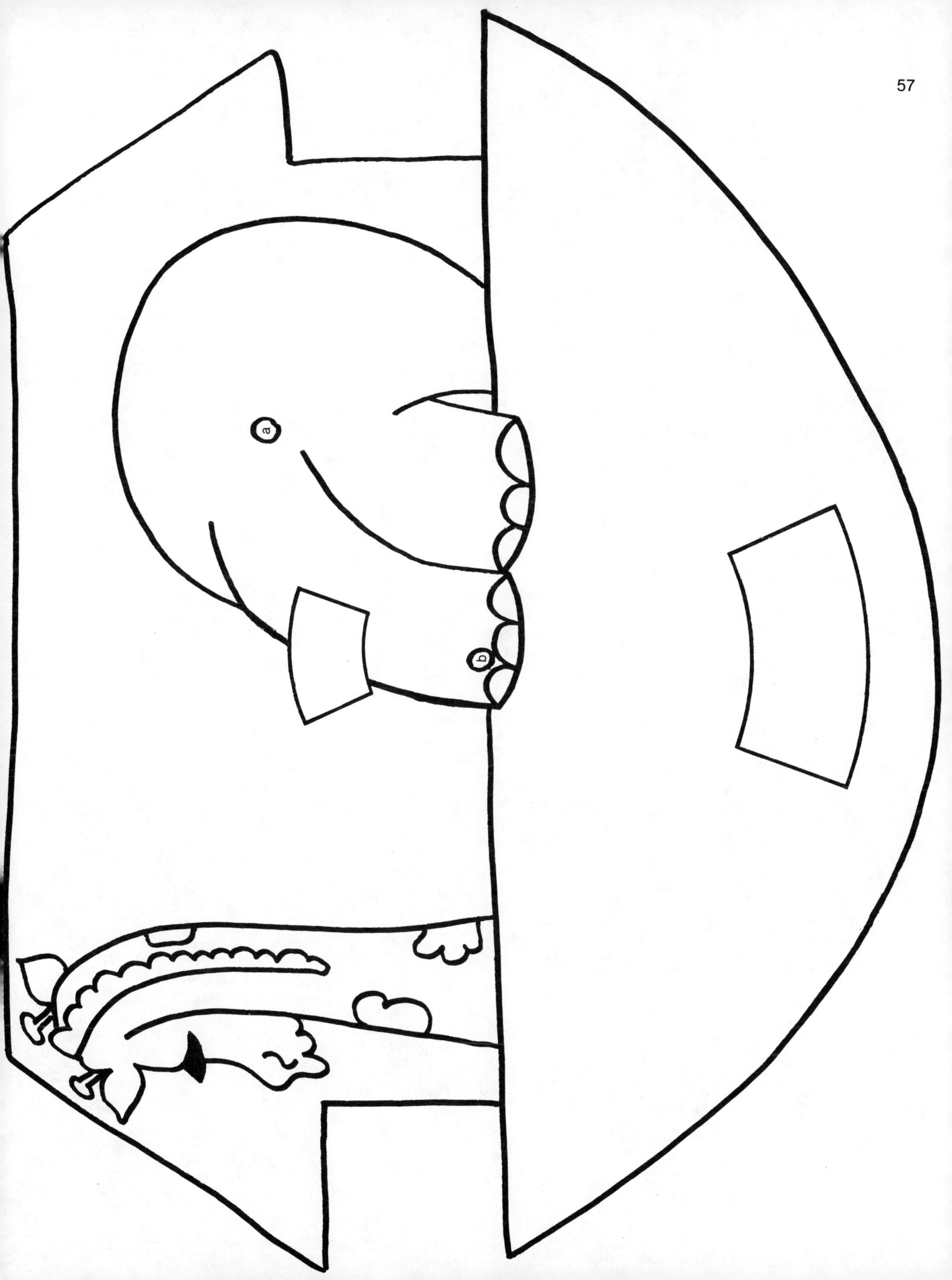
a
b

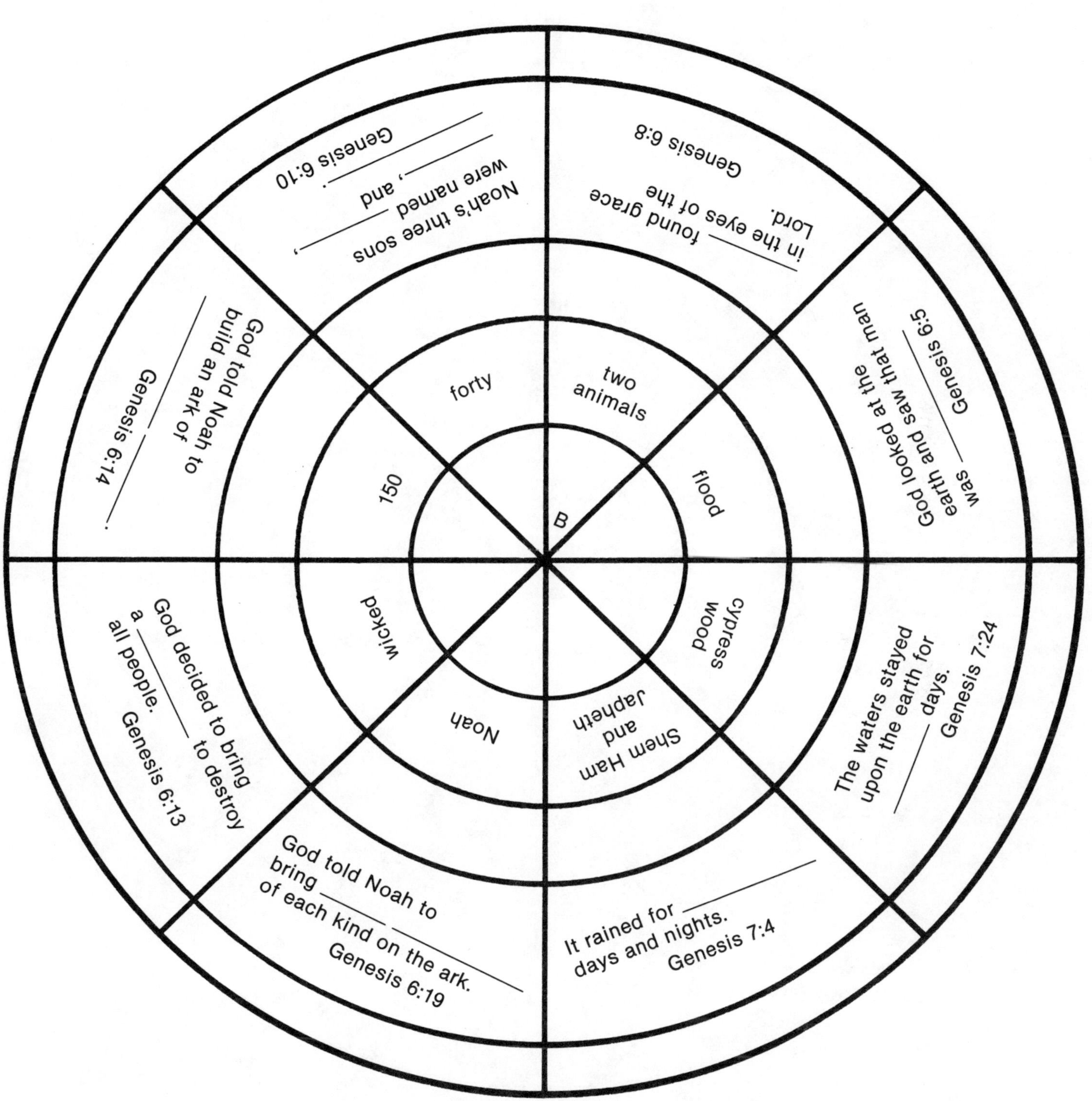

Insert brad 1 through points A. Insert brad 2 through points B.

ADAPTING GAMES

Many games you have at home can be adapted to teach Bible facts. We've all used Concentration and tic-tac-toe and can vouch for their effectiveness with children. Just about any game can be converted, and the children love to use them because they are familiar.

Choose games that have simple instructions and short playing periods. Decide on a subject and make question cards. Be sure to include the Scripture reference. Require the children to answer a question before proceeding with the directions given by the game. Make some provision for the opponent to look up the answer in the Bible and check whether the player's answer is correct.

I pick games at garage sales and use the playing pieces, spinners, and dice with other Bible games. Abandoned game boards are easily made useable by cutting out every other space in the game path and clipping a question sheet underneath. Write questions in each of the empty spaces. Use the instructions for the open-ended game board on page 39 as guidelines.

An old game board is also useful as a reinforced playing surface for a game you make up. Use rubber cement to glue your game board to the more durable surface; then laminate.

Included in the following section are adaptations from checkers, tiddledywinks, and tic-tac-toe. Toys can also be adapted to help a child learn Bible facts. A good example is a wonderful toy called Lite-Brite®. Hasbro Industries has graciously given permission to include games using the Lite-Brite® in this book.

Tic-tac-toe 1

For Two Children or Two Teams

Preparations

1. Find nine pictures that depict nine different stories from the Bible.
2. Cut five squares from red construction paper and five squares from yellow construction paper. Use as markers.

Directions

1. Each team (player) must choose a color to use as markers.
2. Lay the pictures on the table in three rows of three.
3. When it is your turn, choose one of the pictures on the table and tell the Bible story that picture represents.
4. If you can tell something about the picture, you may place your marker on that picture.
5. If you cannot tell about the picture, the opposing team may tell the story and place its marker on the picture.
6. The first team with three markers in a row wins the game.

Tic-tac-toe 2

For Two Children or Two Teams

Preparations

1. Make a tic-tac-toe pattern on a piece of construction paper.
2. Prepare questions from the Bible unit you are studying.

Directions

1. Choose a question.
2. If you can answer the question correctly, you may place your marker on the game board.
3. If you are unable to answer the question, the opposing team may answer the question for you and place its marker on the game board.
4. The first team to place three markers in a row wins the game.

Tiddledywinks

For Two Children or Two Teams

Preparations

1. Prepare a target as shown on page 64.
2. Make 3-by-5 question cards. The questions should be graduated in difficulty. Simple questions are worth 10 points; medium-difficulty questions, 25 points; difficult questions, 100 points.
3. Provide score paper and pencil.

Directions

1. Lay the target on the table.
2. Place the questions on the table in separate piles.
3. Press one penny against another penny to make it flip onto the target.
4. If the penny lands on 10, choose a question from the 10-point pile. If it lands on a 25, choose a 25-point question and so on.
5. The opposing team must look up the answer. If the playing team gives an incorrect answer, the opposing team may read the answer from the Bible for 10 points.
6. The team with the most points at the end of a specific time or the first team to reach a predetermined number of points wins the game.

Tiddledy I.D.

For Two Children or Two Teams

Preparations

Choose 12 Bible pictures for the game. On the pictures write or tape the appropriate Scripture reference. Glue the pictures to a piece of poster board or construction paper.

Directions

1. Play as for the Tiddledywinks game at the top of this page.
2. If your penny lands on a picture, you must give one fact about the picture for 100 points.
3. If you cannot answer the question, your opponent may look up the answer in the Bible and receive 50 points for reading the Scripture verse aloud.
4. The team with the most points at the end of a specified time or the first team to reach a predetermined number of points wins the game.

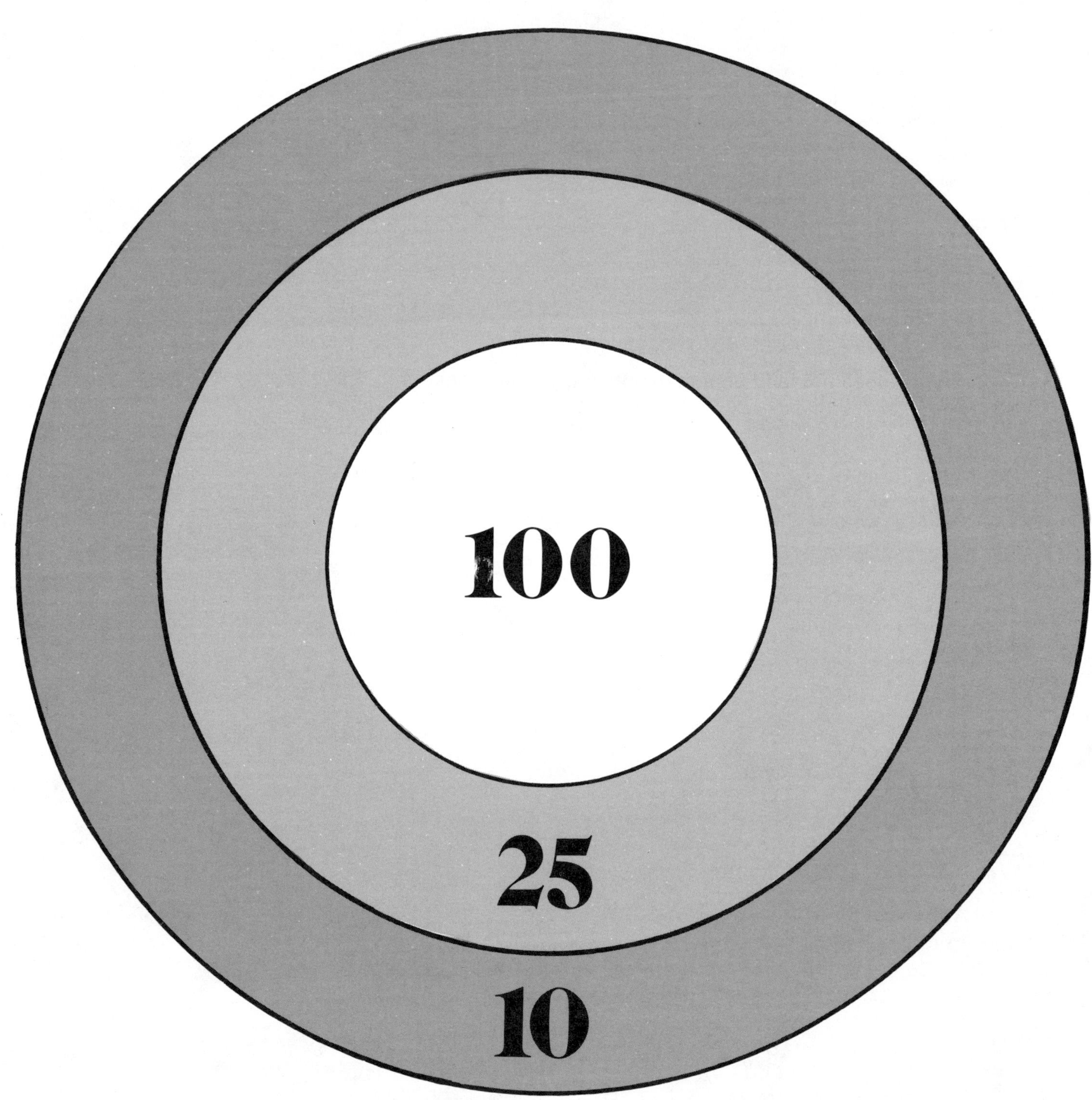

Sample Tiddledywinks target

Map Tiddledy

For Two Children or Two Teams

Preparations

1. Prepare a map of Bible times. (See the New Testament sample on the following page.)
2. Mark the position of Bible places with a letter, but don't identify them by name.
3. Prepare a key.
4. Prepare Bible questions on 3-by-5 cards.

Directions

1. Play as for target tiddledywinks on page 63.
2. If your penny lands on a marked spot, you must identify that place for 100 points.
3. If your penny does not land on a marked spot, you may answer a Bible question for 50 points.
4. If you cannot answer the Bible question, your opponent may look up the answer in the Bible and receive 10 points for reading the answer aloud.
5. Use the key to check map identifications.
6. (Same as the two previous games.)

Map Tiddledy

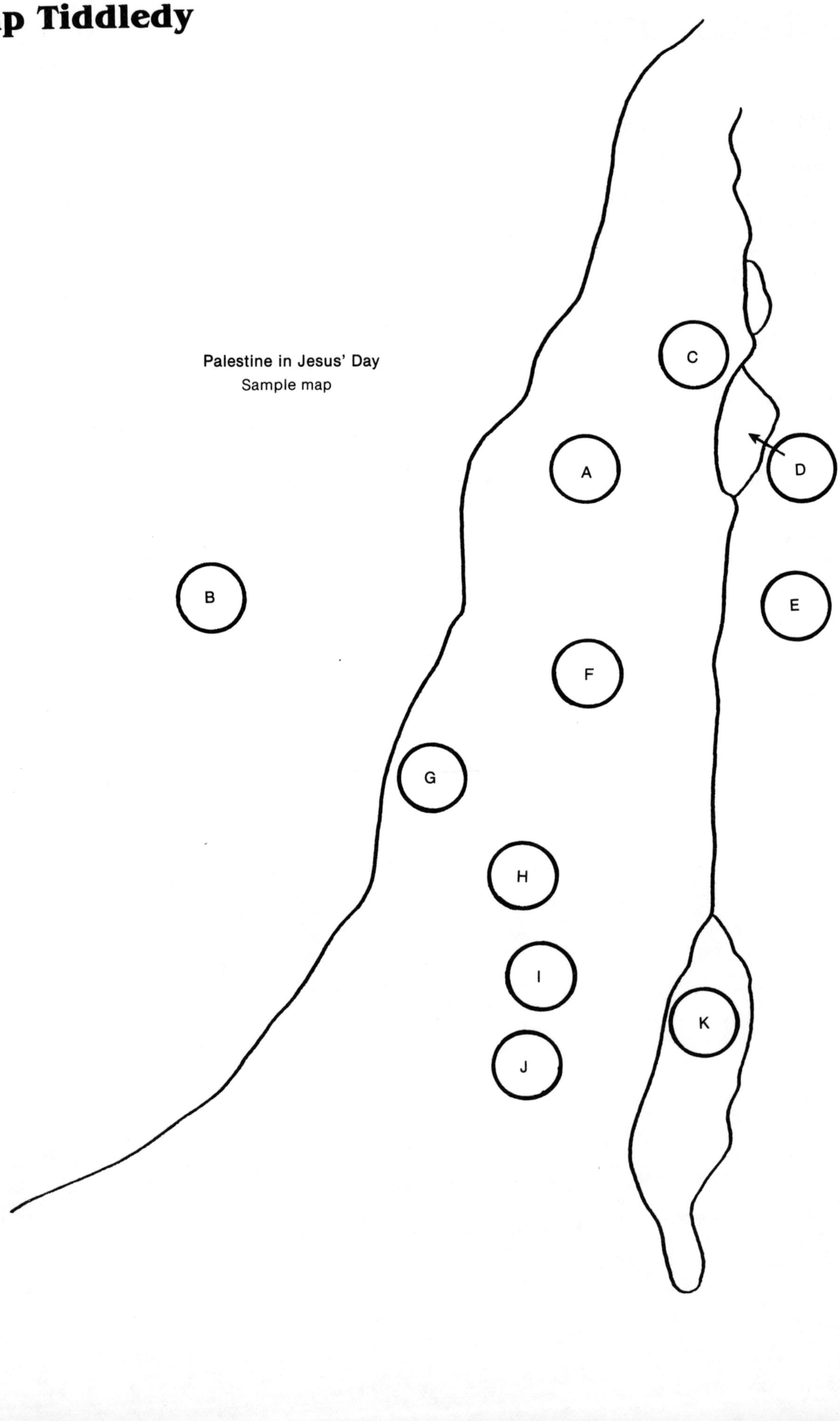

Palestine in Jesus' Day
Sample map

A
B
C
D
E
F
G
H
I
J
K

Key

a. Nazareth
b. Mediterra
Sea
c. Capernau
d. Sea of G
e. Jordan R
f. Samaria
g. Joppa
h. Emmaus
i. Jerusale
j. Bethlehe
k. Dead Se

Checker Switcheroo

For Two Children

Preparations

1. Divide a Bible verse into 12 parts.
2. Make 12 black cards and 12 red cards that are identical in size to the squares on a checkerboard.
3. Write the same Bible verse on the black and red cards.

Directions

1. Each player mixes up his or her cards.
2. Lay the black cards on the red squares and the red cards on the black squares.
3. Take turns moving the cards on your side of the board until the words are in order.
4. You may not move the cards on your opponent's side of the board.
5. You may jump your own cards or move to another space.
6. You may move only one card per turn.
7. The first person to have his or her verse in order wins the game.

Bible Strategy Checkerboard

For Two Children

Preparations

1. Make one red set of 12 cards and one black set of the same number.
2. Divide a Bible verse into four parts.
3. Write one part of the Bible verse on four of the red cards. Put a Bible sticker on the other eight cards. Do the same thing with the black set. Use the same Bible verse.

Directions

1. Place the four parts of the Bible verse on the four black spaces of the checkerboard closest to you.
2. Place the eight Bible squares in front of these.
3. The object of the game is to move the cards with the Bible verses to the opposite side of the board.
4. The blank squares are expendables and are used to protect the Scripture squares.
5. The first player to get his or her four Scripture squares to the opposite side of the board, in order, wins the game.
6. The first player to lose one of the Scripture cards loses the game.

Checker Match-Up

Preparations

1. Prepare 32 cards which list the names of Bible Characters.
2. Prepare 32 cards which list a biography of each character named.

Directions

1. Place 16 name cards on each side of the board.
2. Spread the 32 biography cards face down on the table.
3. Pick up a biography card and try to match it to one of the name cards on your side of the board.
4. If there is a match, place the biography card on top of the name card. If there is no match, return the biography card to its position on the table, face down.
5. The first person to match all of his or her cards wins the game.

Checker Verse Match-Up

Preparations

1. Prepare 32 red squares with one-half of a Bible verse written on each.
2. Prepare 32 white squares with the other half of the Bible verse written on each.

Directions

1. Determine which team is to be white and which team is to be red.
2. Lay the white cards on the table as a draw pile.
3. Lay the red cards on the red squares of the checkerboard.
4. On your turn, draw a card from the pile.
5. Match the Scripture half to one of the Scripture halves on the board. Read the verse aloud.
6. Turn the Scripture verse over. Be sure your color is on top.
7. When all of the Scripture verses have been matched, count how many cards of your color are showing on your opponent's side of the board. You may have 100 points for each of these.
8. Count the cards of your color showing on your side of the board, for 50 points.
9. If your opponent cannot match his Scripture verse, you may answer it for him and receive the points.

Checkerboard Blackout

Preparations

1. Prepare 64 cards that list the books of the Bible.
2. Combine 1 and 2 Corinthians and 1 and 2 Thessalonians.

Directions

1. Shuffle the cards and spread them face up on the table.
2. Open the Bible to the table of contents.
3. Player 1 has five seconds to find as many books of the Bible as he or she can. Start with Genesis. The books must be in order.
4. Place each book in its proper order on the checkerboard, using both the red and black spaces.
5. The second player begins where his opponent left off.
6. Record the number of books each player finds and places on the board in five seconds.
7. The player who places the most cards on the checkerboard wins the game.

Bible-Style Chinese Checkers

For Two Children

Preparations

Make 50 questions. Include the Bible reference on each.

Directions

1. Play as you would Chinese checkers, with the following adaptations.
2. Answer a Bible question before you move a checker.
3. Your opponent must check your answer in the Bible.
4. If the correct answer isn't given, the opponent may read the answer from the Bible and move his marble an extra turn.

LITE-BRITE® GAMES

Lite-Brite® Bible Maps

For One or Two Children

Preparations

1. Make a map of Israel on 9-by-12 construction paper. (Use white chalk on dark colors.)
2. Make a direction card that lists geographical features and cities. Represent each with a different color (see example on page 71). Hang near machine.
3. Make a key.

Directions

1. Insert the map into the machine.
2. The child must place the colored pegs to show where each city on the map is located.

Variation A

1. On the direction card list Bible stories that occurred in different cities, with a Bible reference for each.
2. The child is instructed to place a certain color peg in the spot where the incident occurred.

Variation B

1. The direction card would list Scripture references to Bible cities and places.
2. The child would be instructed to look up the reference.
3. After reading the reference the child would place a peg into the spot on the map mentioned in the Bible verse.

Direction Card for Lite-Brite® Bible Maps

1. Put a green peg where Nazareth is located on the map.
2. Put a white peg where Capernaum is located.
3. Put a gold peg in the Sea of Galilee.
4. Put a blue peg beside the Jordan River.
5. Put a purple peg where Samaria is located.
6. Put a pink peg where Emmaus is located.
7. Put a yellow peg where Bethlehem is located.
8. Put a red and blue peg where Jerusalem is located.
9. Put a red peg where Joppa is located.
10. Put a purple and a pink peg in the Dead Sea.

A Lite-Brite® Bible map for Palestine in Jesus' day might list the geographical features and cities shown on the sample here. See the instructions on page 70.

Lite-Brite® Tac Plus Toe

For Two Children

Preparations

1. Make a tic-tac-toe pattern on 9-by-12 construction paper. Write numbers in the squares as shown in the diagram.
2. Prepare nine question cards. Each card has a number that corresponds to the tic-tac-toe pattern.

Directions

1. The players outline the tic-tac-toe pattern with pegs of the same color.
2. The players each choose a different color as their own.
3. Mix up the question cards.
4. The players take turns answering questions. If the question is answered correctly, they may place a peg in the square with the number that corresponds to the number on question card.
5. Add the numbers you have answered correctly for your score.
6. If you have three pegs in a row at the end of the game, double your score.
7. The player with the highest score wins the game.

5	3	7
2	9	4
8	1	6

Diagram for "Tac Plus Toe" pattern and sample question cards.

5 Naomi and Elimelech went to live in the land of (Moab). Ruth 1:2	3 When Ruth's husband died, she wouldn't leave her mother-in-law, whose name was (Naomi). Ruth 1:8	7 Naomi and Ruth moved to (Bethlehem). Ruth 1:19
2 Ruth gleaned in the fields of a man named (Boaz). Ruth 2:4	9 Poor people were allowed to pick up grain left by the harvest workers. This was called (gleaning). Ruth 2:3	4 Who told Ruth to visit Boaz on the threshing floor? (Naomi). Ruth 3:1–4
8 Ruth married (Boaz) after she moved to Bethlehem. Ruth 4:13	1 Ruth and Boaz had a son named (Obed). Ruth 4:21	6 Ruth was the great-grandmother of (David). Ruth 4:22

Lite-Brite® Bible Books

For Two Children or Two Teams

Preparations

1. Prepunch a subject word, such as the name of a Bible book or a Bible person on a piece of construction paper. (see example on page 75).
2. Use the following directions to make a mask for the word from construction paper. (See example on page 74.)
   - *a.* On a sheet of 9-by-12 construction paper draw a line one inch from the top along the long side of the paper.
   - *b.* Draw vertical lines at one-inch intervals across the long side of the paper.
   - *c.* Number the strips 1—12.
   - *d.* Cut the strips from the bottom of the paper to the line marked at the top of the page. *Do not cut through the horizontal line.*
   - *e.* Make 12 question cards about the subject you chose, but do not ask a question that requires the same answer as the word on the insert. Number the questions 1—12.

Directions

1. Divide into two teams and choose a moderator.
2. Each team chooses a color for their pegs.
3. The moderator puts the answer sheet into the Lite-Brlte®. He replaces the cover and pegs the mask so it covers the answer sheet. Put a peg at the bottom of each strip to hold them in place.
4. The moderator asks team A a question. If team A can answer it, they may pull the peg and lift the strip number that matches the number of the question. Curl the strip upward, reinsert the peg and pin to the top of the machine (See diagram on page 74.)
5. Team A may put their colored pegs in each hole that is exposed to view.
6. If team A cannot answer the question, team B may try. If no one can answer the question, expose the strip and insert neutral color pegs in the holes.
7. The team may try to guess the word at the end of a turn.
8. Continue until one of the teams has guessed the word or until all the strips have been removed. If no one guesses before all the questions are asked, the team with the most colored pegs is the winner. A variation of this is to use maps and picture outlines on the answer sheet.

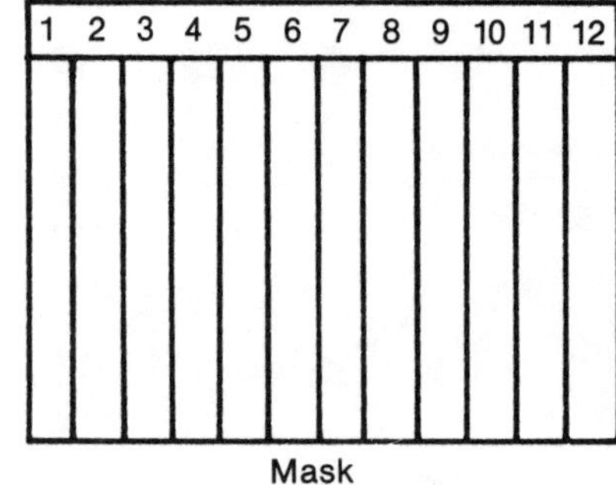

Mask

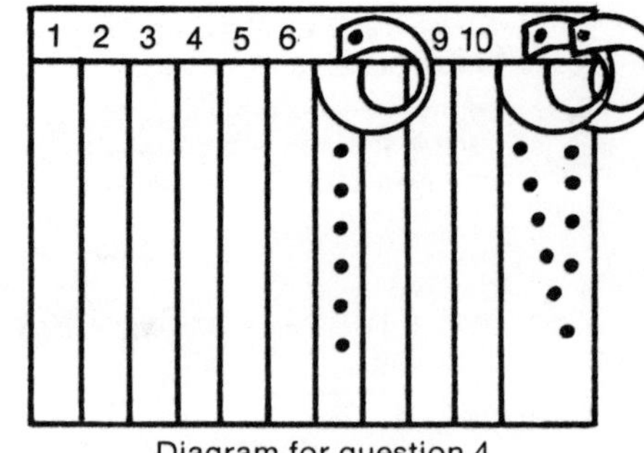

Diagram for question 4

1 Elizabeth and Zechariah were the parents of (John The Baptizer). Luke 1:13	5 When Mary visited Elizabeth, what was her secret? (She was going to be the mother of Jesus.) Luke 1:31	9 John the Baptizer told people that someone special was coming? Who was it? (Jesus.) Matthew 3:11,13
2 What did the angel tell Zechariah? ("You will have a son.") Luke 1:13	6 What message did John the Baptizer preach in the wilderness? (Repent, the kingdom of heaven is at hand.) Matthew 3:2	10 Who came to the Jordan River to be baptised by John? (Jesus.) Matthew 3:13
3 What was the name of the angel? (Gabriel.) Luke 1:19	7 What did John the Baptizer wear? (Clothes of camel hair and a leather girdle.) Matthew 3:4	11 What did John see and hear when he baptised Jesus? (He saw a dove and heard the words "This is My Son in whom I am well pleased.") Matthew 3:17
4 What sign was given to Zechariah? (He was made speechless.) Luke 1:20	8 What did John the Baptizer eat? (Locust and wild honey.) Matthew 3:4	12 Who had John the Baptizer beheaded? (Herod.) Matthew 4:3

Sample pattern for Lite-Brite® Bible Books game. Insert the pattern into the machine and punch the holes before the children play the game.

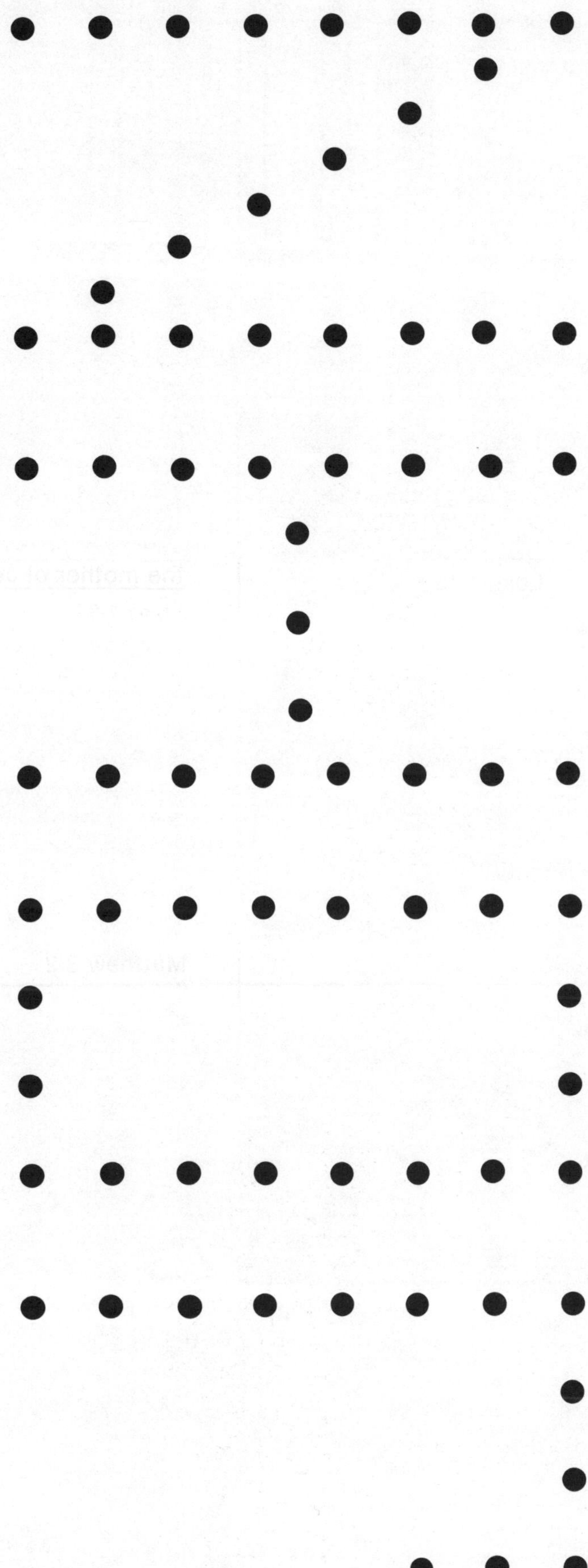

Sample pattern for Lite-Brite® Bible Books game. Insert the pattern into the machine and punch the holes before the children play the game.

Sample pattern for Lite-Brite® Bible Books game. Insert the pattern into the machine and punch the holes before the children play the game.